Discover the
Dinosaurs

DINOSAURS
IN THE SEA

By Joseph Staunton
Illustrated by Luis Rey

amicus
mankato, minnesota

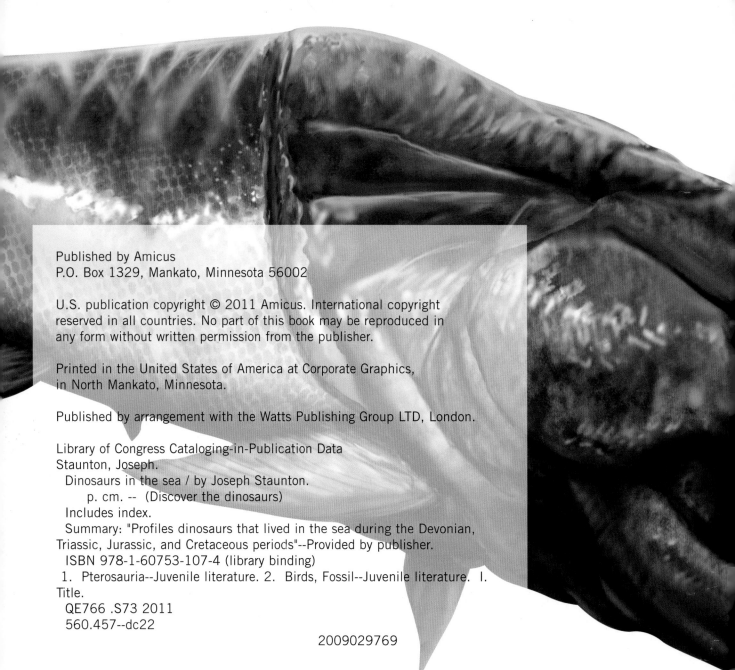

Published by Amicus
P.O. Box 1329, Mankato, Minnesota 56002

Printed in the United States of America at Corporate Graphics,
in North Mankato, Minnesota.

Published by arrangement with the Watts Publishing Group LTD, London.

Library of Congress Cataloging-in-Publication Data
Staunton, Joseph.
  Dinosaurs in the sea / by Joseph Staunton.
      p. cm. -- (Discover the dinosaurs)
  Includes index.
  Summary: "Profiles dinosaurs that lived in the sea during the Devonian,
Triassic, Jurassic, and Cretaceous periods"--Provided by publisher.
  ISBN 978-1-60753-107-4 (library binding)
 1. Pterosauria--Juvenile literature. 2. Birds, Fossil--Juvenile literature. I.
Title.
  QE766 .S73 2011
  560.457--dc22

                                        2009029769

Editor: Jeremy Smith
Design: Nicola Liddiard
Art director: Jonathan Hair
Consultant: Dougal Dixon MSc
Illustrations: Copyright © Luis Rey 2009

1209
32010

9 8 7 6 5 4 3 2 1

Contents

A World of Dinosaurs............................4

Hesperornis 6

Archelon............................8

Tanystropheus 10

Cryptoclidus 12

Dunkleosteus 14

Elasmosaurus 16

Ichthyosaurus............................18

Placodus............................20

Mosasaurus 22

Liopleurodon 24

Quiz............................26

Glossary............................28

Time Line............................31

Index............................32

A World of Dinosaurs

The world we live in is around 4.5 billion years old. Scientists know that there has been life on Earth for around 3.6 billion years because of **fossils** they have found. Most fossils are the remains of animals that lived in the sea.

The Age of Reptiles

Dinosaurs were the most famous group of animals to **evolve** in **prehistoric** times. They were the largest land-living creatures that ever lived. Before, during, and after dinosaurs lived on Earth, there were many strange animals that lived in the sea as well. They all lived in the different periods of time shown in the time line below. Their fossils were found in rocks dating from these different periods.

A Changing World

The Earth in the past looked very different from how it looks now. The layout of the continents and of the oceans was changing all the time. Before the dinosaurs existed, all the continents were jammed together as one big landmass. During dinosaur times, this landmass broke up into the individual continents, which started to move away from each other. This meant that the seas between the continents were opening up. Oceans in other parts of the globe were closing. Changing ocean conditions meant the appearance of new creatures—giant fish, fierce ocean-going reptiles, and even flightless, swimming birds.

Tanystropheus
240 million
years ago

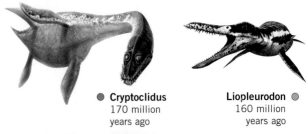

Dunklosteus
370 million
years ago

Placodus
210 million
years ago

Cryptoclidus
170 million
years ago

Liopleurodon
160 million
years ago

millions of years ago

416	251	227	205	180	159
Late	Middle	Upper	Lower	Middle	Upper
DEVONIAN	**TRIASSIC**		**JURASSIC**		

Triassic World There is a single huge landmass. The rest of the world is ocean.

Cretaceous World All the continents are drifting apart. New oceans are forming.

Fossils

Fossils of sea animals are a lot more common than fossils of dinosaurs. Dinosaurs lived on land, and when they died, their bodies rotted in the sun or were eaten by others. When big sea animals died, they were often covered up by **sediment** before they decayed. So people knew about the fossils of sea animals before they knew about the fossils of dinosaurs.

Destruction!

65 million years ago the dinosaurs were wiped out. A giant **meteorite** probably smashed into the Earth. This disaster also wiped out all the sea creatures. But the seas did not stay empty for long. Soon other animals evolved to live in the sea. Today we have whales, seals, penguins, and all kinds of sea animals that are just as strange as those of prehistoric times.

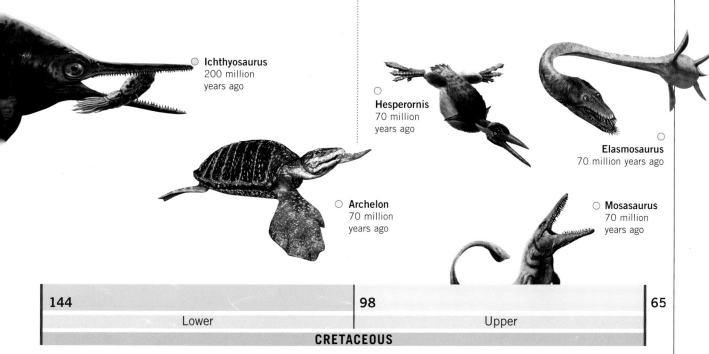

Ichthyosaurus
200 million years ago

Hesperornis
70 million years ago

Elasmosaurus
70 million years ago

Archelon
70 million years ago

Mosasaurus
70 million years ago

144		98		65
	Lower		Upper	
		CRETACEOUS		

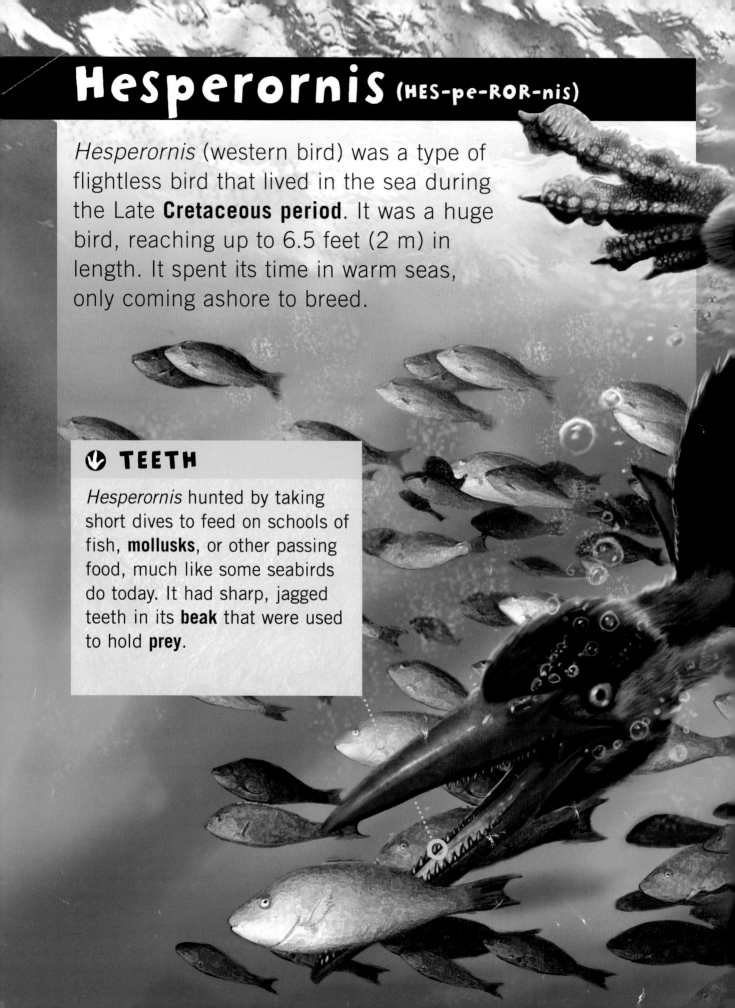

Hesperornis (HES-pe-ROR-nis)

Hesperornis (western bird) was a type of flightless bird that lived in the sea during the Late **Cretaceous period**. It was a huge bird, reaching up to 6.5 feet (2 m) in length. It spent its time in warm seas, only coming ashore to breed.

TEETH

Hesperornis hunted by taking short dives to feed on schools of fish, **mollusks**, or other passing food, much like some seabirds do today. It had sharp, jagged teeth in its **beak** that were used to hold **prey**.

LEGS AND WINGS

Hesperornis had powerful hind legs that it used to dart through the water. It used its tiny wings for steering when diving underwater.

EASY TARGET

Unable to fly or move at more than a hobble on land, *Hesperornis* needed to be wary of **predators** at all times. These included sharks and **plesiosaurs** at sea, and dinosaurs and **pterosaurs** on land and in the air.

Dino-Data

Weight	205 lbs (93 kg)
Length	6.5 feet (2 m)

Archelon (ARE-kell-on)

Archelon (ruling turtle) was a giant turtle that lived during the Late Cretaceous period. Over 13 feet (4 m) long, this reptile could live to an age of 100 years. The first *Archelon* fossil was found in 1895 in South Dakota. An ocean had covered this land during the late Cretaceous period.

 EGGS

Archelon laid its eggs by burying them in sandy beaches at night, just like turtles do today. Its closest living relative is the world's largest turtle, the leatherback sea turtle.

Dino-Data

Weight	4,500 lbs (2,040 kg)
Length	13 feet (4 m)

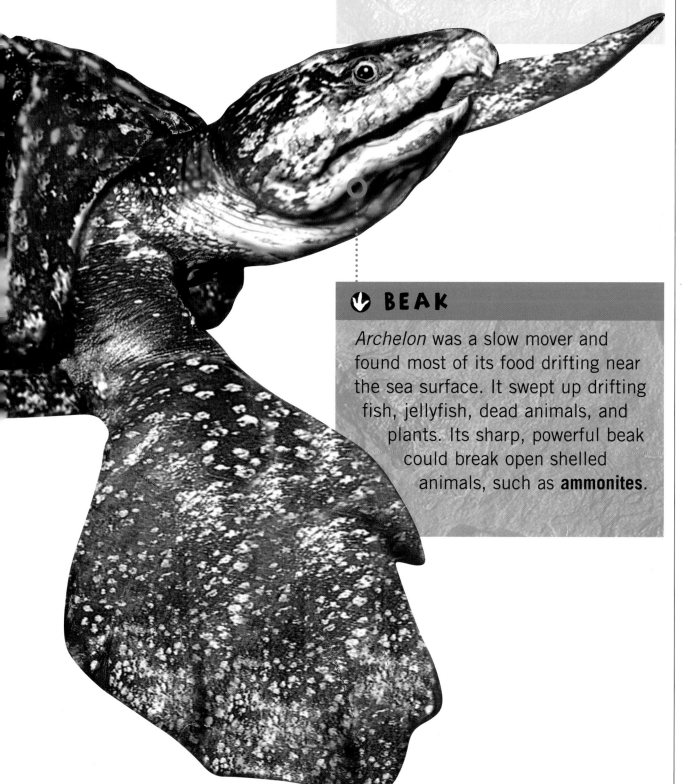

🐾 FLIPPERS

Archelon's huge flippers suggest it was a long-distance swimmer, happiest in the open ocean.

🐾 BEAK

Archelon was a slow mover and found most of its food drifting near the sea surface. It swept up drifting fish, jellyfish, dead animals, and plants. Its sharp, powerful beak could break open shelled animals, such as **ammonites**.

Tanystropheus (TAN-ee-STROH-fee-us)

Tanystropheus (long-necked one) was a reptile that lived in and out of the sea during the **Triassic period** in China, Europe, and the Middle East. It looked like a lizard with a very long neck.

LONG NECK

Tanystropheus had a neck that reached lengths of up to 10 feet (3 m). This was longer than its body and tail combined.

🐾 FISHING

Scientists think that as well as hunting in water, *Tanystropheus* sat on the shoreline and snatched fish and other marine life from the shallows, using its long neck and sharp teeth.

⚘ FEET

Tanystropheus had long, **webbed** feet. These were used for walking and crawling on land and also for swimming fast through the water.

Dino-Data

Weight	309 lbs (140 kg)
Length	16.4 ft (5 m)

Cryptoclidus (crip-toe-CLIDE-us)

Cryptoclidus (hidden collar bone) was a sea-living reptile that looked a bit like a modern seal. It lived in the Middle **Jurassic period**. Its fossils have been found in Britain, France, Russia, and South America.

✪ TEETH

Small fish, squid, and crustaceans like shrimp made up this monster's diet. *Cryptoclidus* caught and sifted prey with its 100 long, pointed teeth.

Dino-Data

Weight	4,400 lbs (2,000 kg)
Length	13 feet (4 m)

↯ SEA AND LAND

It is uncertain whether *Cryptoclidus* spent all its time in the water or some of its time on land. The fact that it looked a little like a seal suggests that it was **amphibious** in nature.

↯ SWIFT MOVER

Despite its size, in the sea *Cryptoclidus* would have moved easily through the water, using all four limbs as paddles, to swim and to hunt its prey.

Dunkleosteus (dunk-ul-AH-stee-us)

Dunkleosteus (Dunkle's bone) was a fearsome prehistoric fish that lived during the Late **Devonian period**. This fish was a ferocious hunter that was unchallenged at the top of the food chain.

❦ MIGHTY BITE

Scientists have worked out that *Dunkleosteus* had the most powerful bite of any fish, more powerful even than a shark. It used its long, bony blades to rip through flesh and bone.

☝ SHAPE

Dunkleosteus was shaped like a shark and was a slow but terrifying hunter. It was powerfully built and its head was protected by armor.

Dino-Data

Weight	5,000 lbs (2,270 kg)
Length	19.6 feet (6 m)

Elasmosaurus (ee-LAS-mo-SAWR-us)

Elasmosaurus (thin-plated lizard) was a Late Cretaceous reptile that lived in the seas of North America. It was capable of swimming thousands of miles through the water using its four flippers.

◑ NECK

Elasmosaurus' neck was much longer than its body. This meant *Elasmosaurus* could attack prey from a distance. It would wait in ambush, then flick out its neck and strike.

☝ BREEDING

Elasmosaurus traveled long distances to find mating and breeding grounds. Most reptiles lay eggs, but *Elasmosaurus* may have given birth to live young, which it cared for until they were old enough to look after themselves.

☝ DIET

Elasmosaurus spent all its time in the water, searching for fish. It would occasionally dive down to the seabed in shallow areas to swallow rounded pebbles, which helped it digest its food and provided **ballast**.

Dino-Data

Weight	4,400 lbs (2,000 kg)
Length	45.9 feet (14 m)

Ichthyosaurus (ICK-thee-oh-SAWR-us)

Ichthyosaurus (fish lizard) darted through European seas during the Jurassic/Early Cretaceous period. It was the first fossil reptile to be discovered. It was found in 1809 by Mary Anning in England and caused a sensation.

☝ SIGHT AND SOUND

Ichthyosaurus had nostrils near its eyes on the top of its head. It had massive ear bones and large eyes, indicating that it probably had very good hearing and keen eyesight.

☝ RELATIVES

Ichthyosaurus was the most common of the ichthyosaur group. It was also quite small. Some of its relatives, however, were as big as whales.

Dino-Data

Weight	440 lbs (200 kg)
Length	6.5 feet (2 m)

⬇ DIET

Ichthyosaurus' diet was mostly made up of fish. However, it could also eat **cephalopods** like these ammonites.

Placodus (PLACK-oh-dus)

Placodus (tablet teeth) was a marine reptile that spent much of its time in shallow seas during the Middle Triassic period. For an animal that lived in the water, it was not that well adapted to the lifestyle. It had small hands and feet, and a long body.

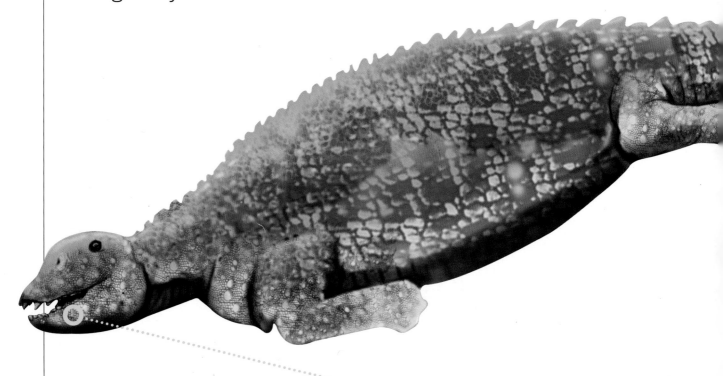

🦷 MOUTH

Placodus's mouth had evolved to eat shellfish. It plucked its prey from the water using its big front teeth and, once in its mouth, ground it to tiny bits using its back teeth.

Dino-Data

Weight	1,700 lbs (800 kg)
Length	10 feet (3 m)

ARMOR

Placodus was heavily built and had thick skin. It looked a bit like an armored crocodile. The thick skin protected *Placodus*, but it also made it very clumsy out of water.

Mosasaurus (MOE-za-SAWR-us)

Mosasaurus (Meuse lizard or river lizard) was a snake-like sea reptile that lived in the seas around present day Holland and other places during the Late Cretaceous period. It was the most fearsome sea predator of its period. *Mosasaurus* was related to modern **monitor lizards**.

⬇ SIZE

The smallest known **mosasaur** was 10 to 11 feet (3 to 3.5 m) long and probably lived in shallow waters near the shore. Larger mosasaurs, such as *Mosasaurus* itself, were more typical, growing to sizes of up to 49 feet (15 m).

↻ AMBUSH!

Mosasaurus was not a fast swimmer. It would have stalked its prey using natural cover provided by seaweed and rocks. Only when prey such as this *Pterodactyl* was within striking range would a *Mosasaurus* propel itself forward. Being caught in its jaws meant almost certain death.

↻ JAWS

Mosasaurus had a double-hinged jaw like that of a snake. This enabled it to gulp down prey almost whole. A skeleton of a *Mosasaurus* has been found in South Dakota that includes the remains of a swallowed *Hesperornis*.

Dino-Data

Weight	28,600 lbs (13,000 kg)
Length	49 feet (15 m)

Liopleurodon (LIE-oh-PLOOR-oh-don)

Liopleurodon (smooth-sided tooth) was a marine reptile that lived in the Jurassic period. Unlike *Elasmosaurus*, this marine reptile had a short neck and a long head. It belonged to the **pliosaur** group, remains of which have been found on every continent.

BIGGEST EVER

The largest complete skeleton of *Liopleurodon* has been found in Mexico. Measuring 65 feet (20 m) from nose to tail, it has been nicknamed the "Monster of Aramberri" after the site in northeastern Mexico where it was dug up.

☙ TEETH

Liopleurodon had a short neck and a very long jaw with rows of teeth. Because of the size and strength of its jaw, *Liopleurodon* could have held a family car in its mouth and broken it in half.

Dino-Data

Weight	9,900 lbs (4,500 kg)
Length	65 feet (20 m)

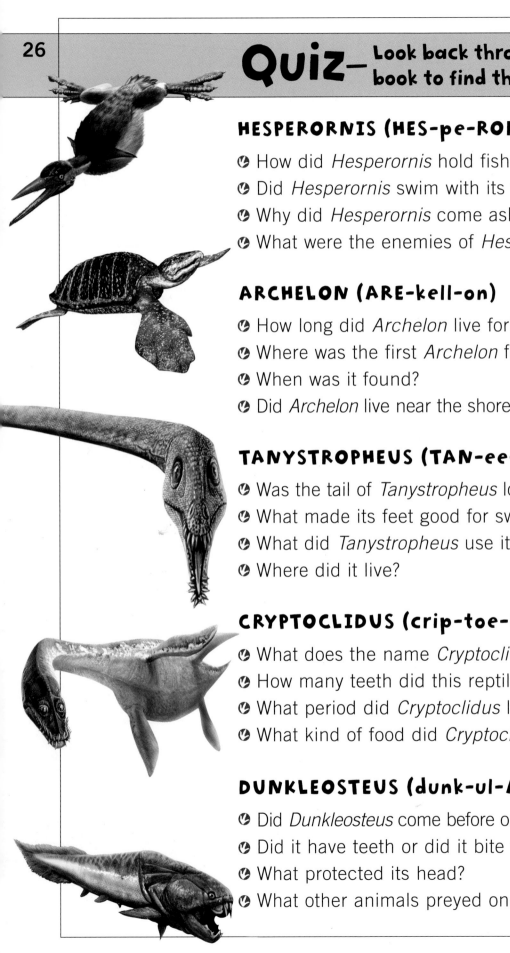

Quiz – Look back through the book to find the answers.

HESPERORNIS (HES-pe-ROR-nis)

☾ How did *Hesperornis* hold fish in its beak?

☾ Did *Hesperornis* swim with its feet or its wings?

☾ Why did *Hesperornis* come ashore?

☾ What were the enemies of *Hesperornis*?

ARCHELON (ARE-kell-on)

☾ How long did *Archelon* live for?

☾ Where was the first *Archelon* fossil found?

☾ When was it found?

☾ Did *Archelon* live near the shore or in the open ocean?

TANYSTROPHEUS (TAN-ee-STROH-fee-us)

☾ Was the tail of *Tanystropheus* longer than the neck?

☾ What made its feet good for swimming?

☾ What did *Tanystropheus* use its long neck for?

☾ Where did it live?

CRYPTOCLIDUS (crip-toe-CLIDE-us)

☾ What does the name *Cryptoclidus* mean?

☾ How many teeth did this reptile have?

☾ What period did *Cryptoclidus* live in?

☾ What kind of food did *Cryptoclidus* eat?

DUNKLEOSTEUS (dunk-ul-AH-stee-us)

☾ Did *Dunkleosteus* come before or after the sea reptiles?

☾ Did it have teeth or did it bite with boney blades?

☾ What protected its head?

☾ What other animals preyed on *Dunkleosteus*?

ELASMOSAURUS (ee-LAS-mo-SAWR-us)

- Why did *Elasmosaurus* have such a long neck?
- Why did *Elasmosaurus* swallow pebbles?
- How many flippers did it have?
- Were its teeth sharp or blunt?

ICHTHYOSAURUS (ICK-thee-oh-SAWR-us)

- What does *Ichthyosaurus* mean?
- Why do you think it has this name?
- Who found the first *Ichthyosaurus*?
- Where was the first *Ichthyosaurus* found?

PLACODUS (PLACK-oh-dus)

- What did *Placodus* eat?
- Did it live in deep or shallow water?
- How long was *Placodus*?
- How many kinds of teeth did it have?

MOSASAURUS (MOE-za-SAWR-us)

- What is the nearest modern relative of *Mosasaurus*?
- Did it chew its food?
- How do we know that it ate birds?
- Did *Mosasaurus* chase its prey or ambush it?

LIOPLEURODON (LIE-oh-PLOOR-oh-don)

- What do we call the group of animals to which *Liopleurodon* belonged?
- Where was the biggest found?
- Did it have a long or a short neck?
- When did *Liopleurodon* live?

Glossary

Ammonite: A prehistoric cephalopod, like an octopus inside a coiled shell.

Amphibious: Able to live on both land and water, like a frog.

Ballast: Stones or other heavy weights used to keep a floating object, like a fish or a swimming animal, stable.

Beak: A lightweight, hard structure on the mouths of birds or turtles.

Cephalopod: A mollusk that has a bunch of tentacles around its mouth, like an octopus or a squid.

Cretaceous period: A period of the Earth's history from 144–65 million years ago.

Crustacean: A group of aquatic creatures that includes lobsters, crabs, shrimps, and barnacles.

Devonian period: A period of time, 405–345 million years ago, when fish dominated and amphibians and ammonites began to emerge.

Evolve: To change from one form to another over time and over many generations.

Fossil: The remains of a prehistoric animal or plant that has been turned to stone and preserved for millions of years.

Jurassic period: A period of Earth's history from 205–144 million years ago.

Meteorite: A lump of rock floating in space that can sometimes fall through the atmosphere and crash into the Earth.

Mollusk: One of a group of animals usually living in the water and usually covered by a shell. Clams and snails are mollusks.

Monitor lizard: A type of large lizard. The biggest lizard living today, the Komodo dragon, is a monitor.

Mosasaur: A type of large swimming lizard that lived in the sea in Cretaceous times.

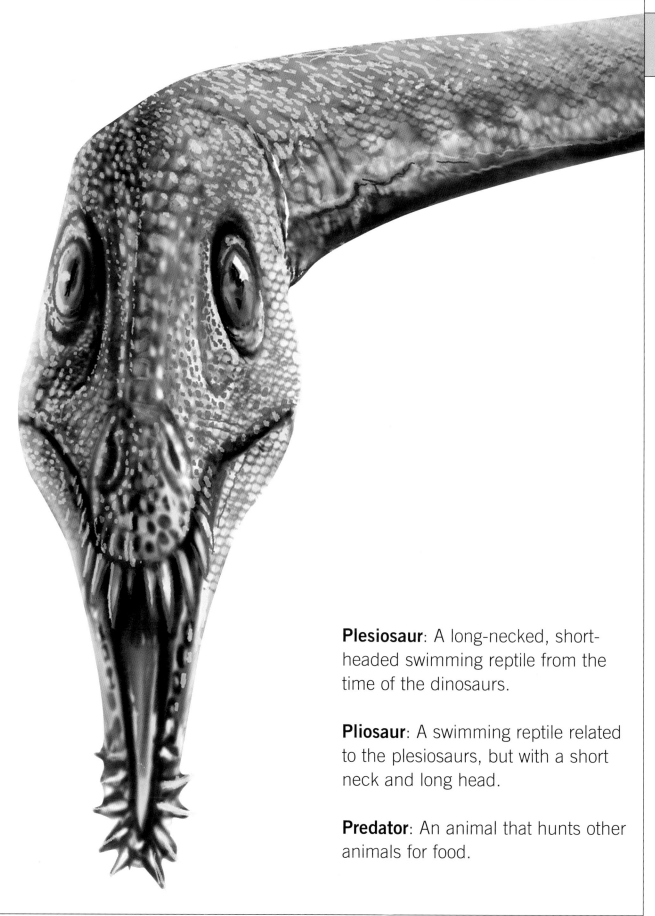

Plesiosaur: A long-necked, short-headed swimming reptile from the time of the dinosaurs.

Pliosaur: A swimming reptile related to the plesiosaurs, but with a short neck and long head.

Predator: An animal that hunts other animals for food.

Prehistoric: Before written history.

Prey: An animal that is hunted by another animal, a predator, for food.

Pterosaur: A kind of flying reptile from the age of the dinosaurs.

Triassic period: A period of Earth's history from 251–205 million years ago.

Webbed: Having flaps of skin between the toes to help in swimming. A duck has webbed feet.

Earth's Time Line

The history of the Earth dates back over 4 billion years. Scientists divide this time into periods. The earliest period of time is the Cambrian period. Dinosaurs appeared on Earth from the Triassic to the Cretaceous periods. Mammals, including humans, appeared in the Quarternary period.

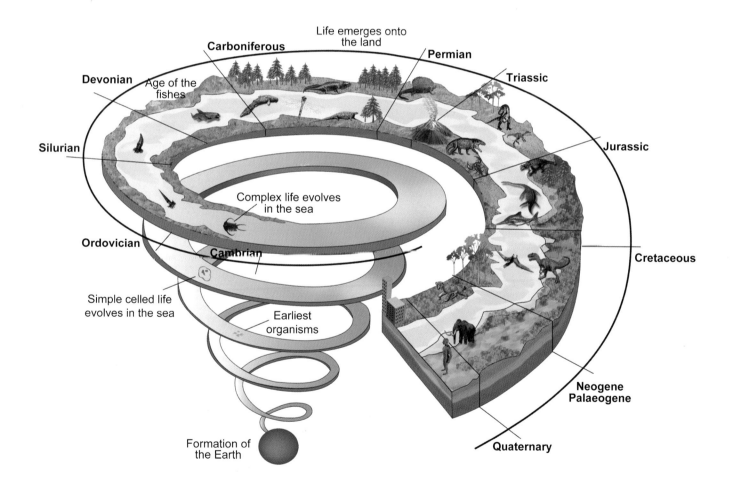

Index

A-B
ammonites 9, 11, 19, 21
amphibious creatures 15
Anning, Mary 18
Archelon 5, 8, 9
armor 15, 21
ballast 17
beak 6, 9
birds 4, 6
breeding 6, 17

C-D
cephalopods 19
China 10
Cretaceous period 6, 8, 18, 22
Cryptoclidus 4, 12, 13
Devonian period 4, 14
digestion 17, 19
dinosaurs 4, 5, 7
Dunkleosteus 14, 15

E-F
ears 18
eggs 8, 17

Elasmosaurus 16, 17, 24
Europe 10, 18
eyes 18
feet 7, 11, 20
fish 4, 6, 9, 10, 12, 14, 17, 18, 19, 20
flippers 9, 16
food 6, 9, 14, 17
food chain 14
fossils 4, 5, 12, 18

G-H
Hesperornis 5, 6, 7, 23

I-K
Ichthyosaurus 5, 18, 19
jaws 23, 25
Jurassic period 12, 18, 24

L-N
legs 7
Liopleurodon 4, 24, 25
Middle East 10
mollusks 6
Mosasaurus 5, 22, 23
neck 10, 16, 24, 25
North America 16
nostrils 18

O-Q
ocean 4, 5, 8, 9
Placodus 4, 20, 21
plants 9
plesiosaurs 7
pliosaurs 24
predators 7, 22
prey 6, 12, 13, 16, 20, 23
pterosaurs 7

R-S
reptiles 4, 8, 10, 12, 16, 17, 18, 20, 22, 24
seas 4, 5, 6, 7, 9, 10, 12, 13, 16, 18, 20, 22
skeleton 23, 24
South America 12
swimming 4, 9, 11, 13, 16, 23

T-U
tail 10, 24
Tanystropheus 4, 10, 11
teeth 6, 10, 12, 20, 25
Triassic period 4, 10, 20
turtles 8, 21

V-Z
wings 7